# TUDOR AND STUART FABRICS

# THE WORLD'S HERITAGE OF WOVEN FABRICS

*Under the General Editorship of* CYRIL G. E. BUNT

*VENETIAN FABRICS*

*THE SILKS OF LYONS*

*SICILIAN AND LUCCHESE FABRICS*

*TUDOR AND STUART FABRICS*

*CHINESE FABRICS*

*PERSIAN FABRICS*

*FLORENTINE FABRICS*

*SPANISH SILKS*

*HISPANO-MORESQUE FABRICS*

*BYZANTINE FABRICS*

*THE FABRICS OF PERU*

Other volumes are to follow and will be announced from time to time

# TUDOR & STUART FABRICS

*by*

## CYRIL G. E. BUNT

F. LEWIS, PUBLISHERS, LTD.
LEIGH-ON-SEA

PRINTED AND MADE IN ENGLAND

©

Copyright F. Lewis, Publishers, Ltd.
The Tithe House, Leigh-on-Sea
England

First published in 1961

Produced for and under the supervision of the
Publishers at The Dolphin Press, Brighton.
Bound by A. W. Bain and Co. Ltd., London

# Tudor & Stuart Fabrics

THE BEGINNING of the silk-weaving industry in England may be dated somewhere in the mid-fourteenth century. At first it was confined to the making of small articles, since no piece silk was woven and what was obtained was imported. In those early days, moreover, the weavers were mostly foreigners. There is record of one Peter le Roye being summoned for unauthorized silk-weaving at Bermondsey, and in Southwark some years later Burgundian, French and Dutch weavers are mentioned in the Returns of Aliens.

There are records of foreign weavers in London so early as 1618, but the imports of taffetas, velvets, figured satins and other silk goods was by no means confined to the Capital. Norwich is one centre mentioned in 1602 when Francis Smalpiece refers to 'Norwich Satyns, Spanish Satyns whereof the greatest parte ys sylke . . . (or) Tobyns, half sylks'.

Queen Elizabeth in that year (1602) is alleged to have lost revenue by reason that strangers were producing 'tuft-taffetas, velvets, figured satins and other silk and wool goods'.

In those days raw silk, like piece goods, was imported. None was home produced for the climate was found to be unfavourable to the cultivation of the mulberry. However, the throwsters of London formed themselves into a corporation in 1629, and thirty years later it is recorded that forty thousand men and women were employed in the industry. We may presume this figure included the weavers.

One hardly need mention that the Tudors loved fine clothes, especially silks, of which contemporary portraits give us ample proof, if not the prolific dramatic literature of the age of Shakespeare. Sarcenet and cypress, taffetas and floral damasks, to say nothing of the magnificent cloths of gold, silver tinsel and tissue. The drama of the period, having little in the way of stage-setting, depended all the more upon sumptuous raiment to suggest pomp and circumstance. Much gold and silver, or perhaps tinsel, was employed in the revels; and in such plays as *Much Ado about Nothing* and *Anything for a Quiet Life* it is the cloth of gold and silver which are used to suggest opulence.

The variety of rich silken fabrics included many whose names are now unfamiliar except for the texts in which they are mentioned. One such was Bodkin, or Baudkin, first known in England in the fifteenth century. It was an ancient fabric, not only silken, in raised pattern, but especially rich in cloths of gold. Another was Tabine, a product of Norwich, at the beginning of the seventeenth century. Beloved by contemporary ladies, and Queen Elizabeth's new year gifts in 1600 included many articles in Tabine ('silver tabyne, gold-tabyne, etc.').

'Tissue', a word much used in museum description, and so familiar, was much favoured by Royalty. We have only to consult the Costume Accounts of Henry VIII and his wives to find it often specified. It was used as hangings and, indeed, as a stage detail of *decor* it was an indication of wealth.

Damask is again familiar, but not so Cypress, a thin fabric of silk and linen, transparent and used much as a veiling. Plushes and velvets were among the more expensive fabrics and most, if not all, types of velvet were imported (from Genoa, Lucca and Florence). Velvet upon velvet, double pile, has rightly been termed 'incomparable' for its effective beauty. In 1599 Queen Elizabeth received as a new year present a mantle 'of ash-coloured and heare-coloured unshorne velvet lozenwise, lyned with crimson unshorne velvet'.

Velvets were frequently enriched with embroidery in flowers, or 'branched', and by the addition of tiny loops of gold thread in patterns over the whole surface. In the accounts the latter is often referred to as 'pirled'.

The sixteenth century may well be called the age of embroidered costume, its phenominal rise to popularity being ascribed by some authors to the re-introduction of the manufacture of fine Spanish needles by Christopher Greening in 1560. But, as has rightly been observed, the rage for all-over work cannot be credited to this alone. Spanish influence played its part also, for there are numerous references in wardrobe accounts to 'Spanish workes'.

Chiefly these were in needlework on fine imported linen, in silks of various colours and threads of metal. A speciality of the era was known as 'block work'.

The reign of Elizabeth saw an immense amount of ecclesiastical embroidery turned to lay uses, ruthlessly altered to provide personal and household decoration. Particular mention may perhaps be made of the capacious copes and other vestments which were altered to cushion covers or garments and, too often, burned for sake of the precious gold with which they were woven.

Rich as these were, they were frequently embellished with cunning embroidery, and towards the close of the century the floral, animal and insect motifs became popular.

We recall mention of gowns of cloth of silver decorated with 'workes of yellow silk like flies, worms and snailes'.

It was an age of emblems inspired by the rare work by Whitney, 'The Choice of Emblems'. Many of these embroideries were inspired by woven fabrics, for it would seem that many of the craftsmen and needlewomen who had lost their ecclesiastical patronage served in domestic employment.

The patterns characteristic of the reign of Elizabeth were continued in the Jacobean era, quite as clever, but less graceful and stiff in design.

Any representative collection of Tudor fabrics must include a number of garments of both men and women; especially rich were the kirtle, or gown, with its 'pair' of bodies, the stomacher or 'forepart' of the women; the doublet hose, canons and galligascons of the men.

The transition in style between Tudor and Stuart design is clearly defined; but, none the less, to set definite limits of demarkation between the two is not quite so easy. There is inevitable overlap, which is quite demonstrable in the case of woven and embroidered fabrics, even as it is in furniture. There is, as always, the era of transition, and one cannot detect (nor should we expect) a sudden change just because Queen Elizabeth died and the Royal line of Stuarts ascended the throne. Moreover there was the economic factor to be taken into consideration. The fabrics of those days were woven to withstand longer and harder use than those of today and, economically, this was controlled by the inherently expensiveness of raw material.

Rich velvets, heavy damasks and stout silks were expensive and were, to a great extent, imported from the Continent, although the weaving of silk had already been established in England. In consequence they were expected to last, and Elizabethan draperies and hangings were not discarded just because James came to the throne of the two kingdoms or Charles II came back from France to restore the Monarchy after the stultifying wave of Puritanism had discouraged the weaving of fine, sumptuary fabrics.

Nevertheless the effect of the Restoration introduced a spirit of buoyancy and reflected a lightness of fancy into the textile design which is readily identified as contrasted with the greater part of Tudor textiles.

Transition, when it does come, is of course gradual. Especially in those days designers were not limited to up-to-date motives. They could not help drawing upon the already existing designs. But they eventually achieved stylistic originality, although this very originality was presumably built upon the flora and fauna already in vogue in the Tudor stuffs, based upon favourites of Elizabethan gardens or perpetuated in flower-pieces of the older painters, woodcutters, etc. Gerard's *Herbal*, published in 1597, and Gesner's *Catalogus Plantarum* of 1542, and his *Historia Animalium* of 1558, were drawn upon for inspiration in the production of those celebrated Pattern Books, of which Shorleyber's *A Schole Howse for the Needle* is a rare and interesting survival. The latter was published in 1632 and no complete copy is known to exist.

These pattern books were only compendiums of units of design and, passing from hand to hand, had a most definite formative influence upon the designs of the subsequent years of the seventeenth century.

It may be surmised, as already hinted, that the sombre Puritan period, with its utilitarian urge, was superseded by a period of frank enjoyment which was reflected in the increased flippancy and brighter colourings of the typical Jacobean fabrics—so important an adjunct to the pleasure-seeking spirit of Restoration times. It was contributory to the general frivolity of the era, and yet there was little frivolous in the resulting artistic effect, as the illustrations given in this volume will abundantly testify.

CYRIL G. E. BUNT

ILLUSTRATIONS

FIG. I. NEEDLEWORK BAG. circa 1450
COURTESY OF VICTORIA & ALBERT MUSEUM, LONDON

FIG. 2. EMBROIDERED LINEN JACKET. LATE 16TH OR EARLY 17TH CENTURY
COURTESY OF THE METROPOLITAN MUSEUM OF ART, ROGERS FUND, 1923

FIG. 3. MAN'S CAP. 16TH CENTURY
COURTESY OF SIR JOHN CAREW POLE, BART

FIGURE 4. EMBROIDERED PANEL. 16TH CENTURY
COURTESY OF SIR JOHN CAREW POLE, BART

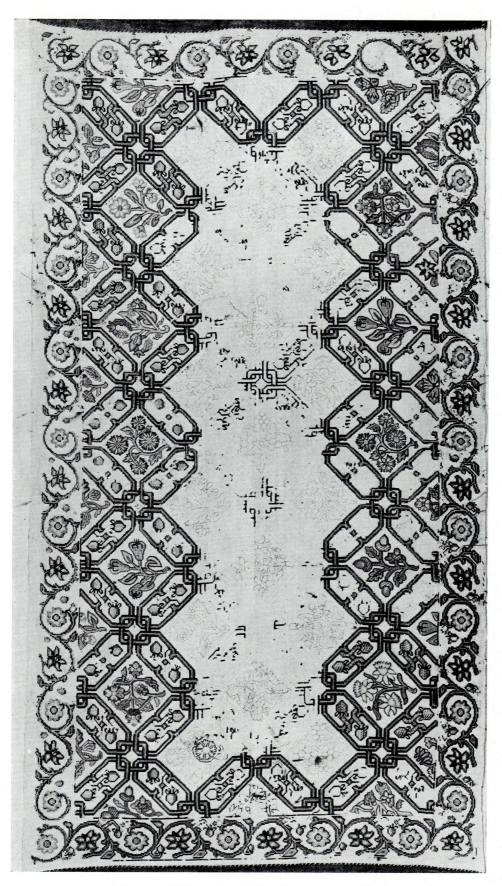

FIG. 5. EMBROIDERED PANEL (UNFINISHED) 16TH CENTURY
COURTESY OF SIR JOHN CAREW POLE, BART

FIG. 6. EMBROIDERED PANELS. SECOND HALF 16TH CENTURY
COURTESY OF THE DUKE OF DEVONSHIRE

FIG. 7. EMBROIDERED HANGING. FIGURES OF SCIENCES. SECOND HALF 16TH CENTURY
COURTESY OF THE DUKE OF DEVONSHIRE

FIG. 8. EMBROIDERED PANELS. SECOND HALF 16TH CENTURY
COURTESY OF THE DUKE OF DEVONSHIRE

FIG. 9. SAMPLER DESIGNS FOR EMBROIDERY. circa 1600
COURTESY OF SIR JOHN CAREW-POLE, BART

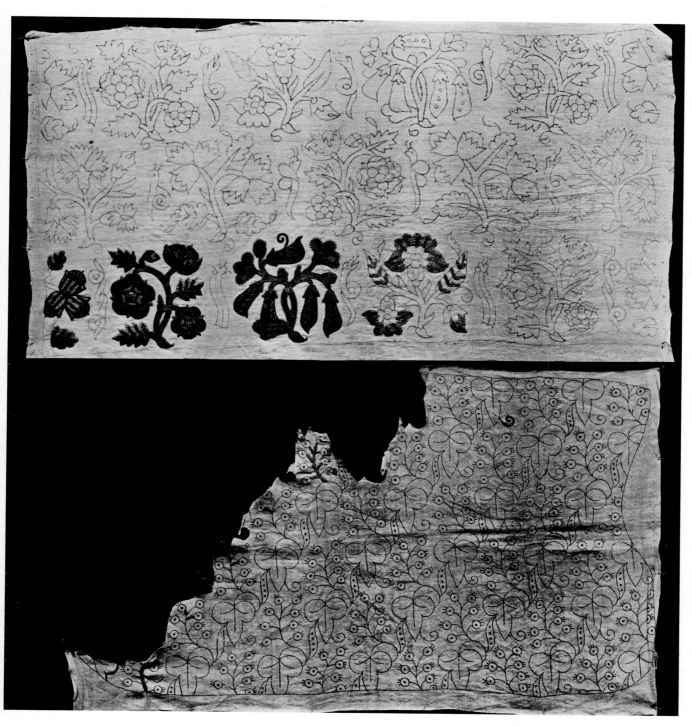

FIG. 10/11. CUSHION COVERS (UNFINISHED) 16TH CENTURY
COURTESY OF SIR JOHN CAREW POLE, BART

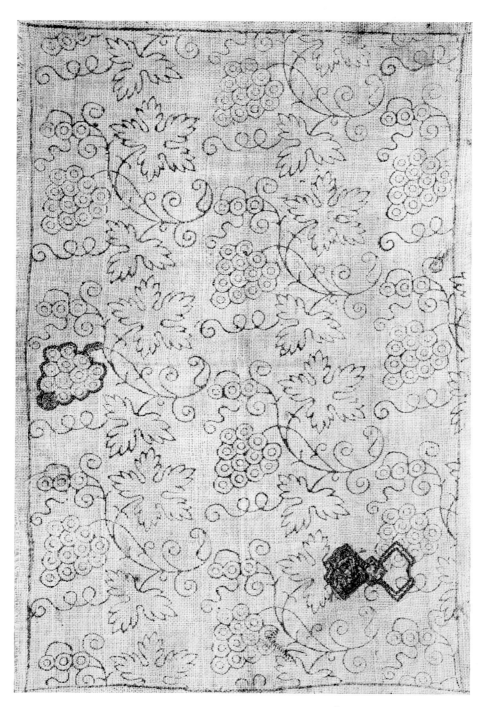

FIG. 12. CUSHION COVER (UNFINISHED) 16TH CENTURY
COURTESY OF SIR JOHN CAREW POLE, BART

FIG. 13. CANVAS WORK EMBROIDERY. 16TH CENTURY
COURTESY OF THE VICTORIA & ALBERT MUSEUM, LONDON

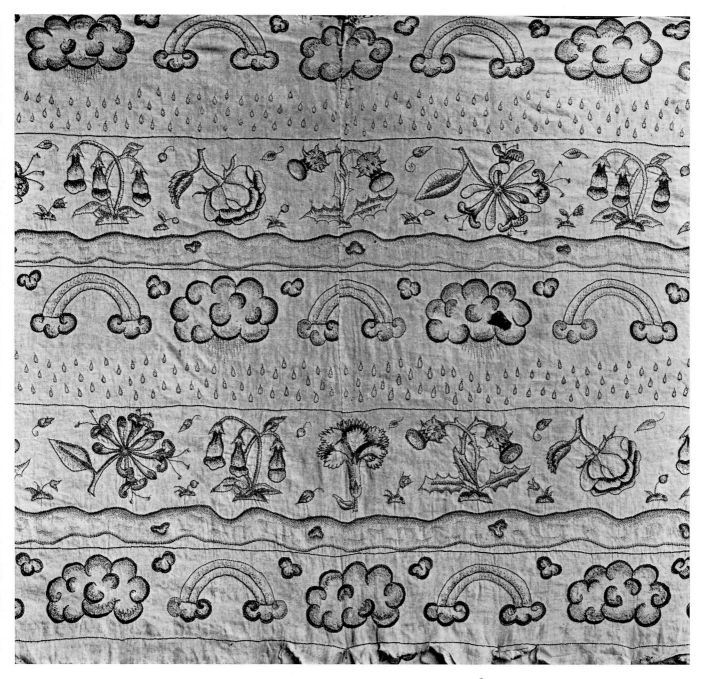

FIG. I4. PORTION OF EMBROIDERED TUNIC. LATE I6TH CENTURY
COURTESY OF LADY STANLEY OF ALDERLEY

FIG. 15. PILLOW CASE IN PETIT POINT. 16TH CENTURY
COURTESY OF SIR JOHN CAREW POLE, BART

FIG. 16. EMBROIDERED LINEN (BLACKWORK) LATE 16TH CENTURY
COURTESY OF THE METROPOLITAN MUSEUM OF ART, ROGERS FUND, 1935

FIG. 17/18/19. THREE EMBROIDERED PANELS. 16TH CENTURY
COURTESY OF CROFTON CROXALL ESQ.

FIG. 20. COVERLET. 16TH CENTURY
COURTESY OF THE VICTORIA & ALBERT MUSEUM, LONDON

FIG. 21. CUSHION COVER. LATE 16TH CENTURY
COURTESY OF THE VICTORIA & ALBERT MUSEUM, LONDON

FIG. 22. EMBROIDERED TABLE COVER (PORTION) LATE 16TH CENTURY. SIZE: 13′ × 6′
COURTESY OF THE VICTORIA & ALBERT MUSEUM, LONDON

FIG. 23/24. TAPESTRY HANGINGS. LATE 16TH CENTURY
COURTESY OF THE VICTORIA & ALBERT MUSEUM, LONDON

FIG. 25/26 *(top)* BOOK: *De Antiquitate Britannicae Ecclesiae* by Parker. 1572
COURTESY THE BRITISH MUSEUM, LONDON
*(Bottom)* EMBROIDERED BOOK COVER. LATE 16TH CENTURY
COURTESY OF THE VICTORIA & ALBERT MUSEUM, LONDON

FIG. 27. EMBROIDERED COVER. LATE 16TH CENTURY
COURTESY OF MISS HANNA

FIG. 28. LINEN PILLOW CASE EMBROIDERED BLACK SILK. 16TH CENTURY
COURTESY OF THE VICTORIA & ALBERT MUSEUM

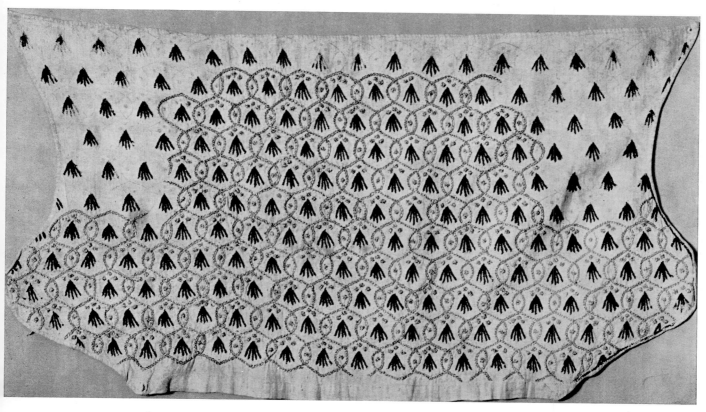

FIG. 29. WOMAN'S HEADDRESS, EMBROIDERED LINEN. LATE 16TH OR EARLY 17TH CENTURY
COURTESY OF THE METROPOLITAN MUSEUM OF ART, ROGERS FUND, 1936

FIG. 30. PIECE OF EMBROIDERED SATIN BED-HANGING. LATE 16TH CENTURY
COURTESY OF THE METROPOLITAN MUSEUM OF ART, ROGERS FUND, 1920

FIG. 31. PETIT POINT PANEL (LUCRETIAS BANQUET). LATE 16TH CENTURY
COURTESY OF THE VICTORIA & ALBERT MUSEUM, LONDON

FIG. 32/33. *(top)* EMBROIDERED COVER. EARLY 17TH CENTURY
*(bottom)* TAPESTRY (portion only) SECOND HALF 17TH CENTURY
COURTESY VICTORIA & ALBERT MUSEUM, LONDON

FIG. 34. BROCADED SILK TISSUE. ENGLISH OR FRENCH 17TH CENTURY
COURTESY VICTORIA & ALBERT MUSEUM, LONDON

FIG. 35/36. *(top)* PANEL WITH DESIGN IN INK. EARLY 17TH CENTURY
*(bottom)* PANEL. LINEN & COTTON. EMBROIDERED COLOURED WORSTEDS. LATE 17TH CENTURY
COURTESY VICTORIA & ALBERT MUSEUM, LONDON

FIG. 37. CARPET. (CENTRE PORTION). FIRST HALF 17TH CENTURY
COURTESY OF LORD SACKVILLE

FIG. 38. SAMPLER. 1630
COURTESY OF DORSET COUNTY MUSEUM, DORCHESTER

FIG. 39. LINEN: BLOCK PRINTED. EARLY 17TH CENTURY
COURTESY VICTORIA & ALBERT MUSEUM, LONDON

FIG. 40. LINEN: PLATE PRINTED IN BLACK. EARLY 17TH CENTURY
COURTESY VICTORIA & ALBERT MUSEUM

FIG. 41. EMBROIDERED HANGING. EARLY 17TH CENTURY
COURTESY VICTORIA & ALBERT MUSEUM, LONDON

FIG. 42. PURSES & PART OF BED HANGING. EARLY 17TH CENTURY
COURTESY OF VICTORIA & ALBERT MUSEUM, LONDON

FIG. 43. PART OF HANGING. WOOL EMBROIDERY ON COTTON & LINEN. MID. 17TH CENTURY
COURTESY OF VICTORIA & ALBERT MUSEUM, LONDON. (GIFT OF G. BARON ASH)

FIG. 44. EMBROIDERED PANEL. 17TH CENTURY
COURTESY OF VICTORIA & ALBERT MUSEUM, LONDON

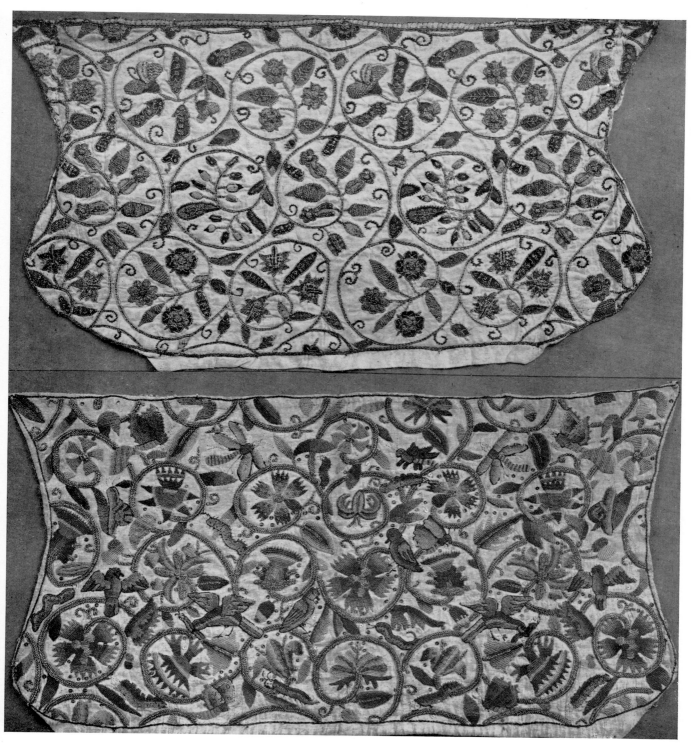

FIG. 45/46. COIFS. LATE 17TH CENTURY
COURTESY OF SIR WILLIAM LAWRENCE

FIG. 47. CURTAIN: WOOL ON COTTON & LINEN. SECOND HALF 17TH CENTURY
COURTESY OF VICTORIA & ALBERT MUSEUM, LONDON

FIG. 48. VALENCE. WOOL ON COTTON & LINEN. SECOND HALF 17TH CENTURY
COURTESY OF VICTORIA & ALBERT MUSEUM, LONDON

FIG. 49. EMBROIDERED HANGING (CREWEL WORK) LATE 17TH CENTURY
COURTESY VICTORIA & ALBERT MUSEUM

FIG. 50. PART OF SET OF BED HANGINGS. LATE 17TH CENTURY
COURTESY VICTORIA & ALBERT MUSEUM, LONDON

FIG. 51. CURTAIN (PART OF) WOOL ON COTTON & LINEN. MID. 17TH CENTURY
COURTESY OF VICTORIA & ALBERT MUSEUM, LONDON

FIG. 52. HANGING. WOOL ON LINEN & COTTON. LATE 17TH CENTURY
COURTESY OF VICTORIA & ALBERT MUSEUM, LONDON

FIG. 53. A JACOBEAN PANEL, IN BRILLIANT COLOURED WOOL
COURTESY OF LADY JANE RICHMOND

FIG. 54. HANGING (CREWEL WORK). circa 1680
COURTESY OF VICTORIA & ALBERT MUSEUM, LONDON

FIG. 55. JACOBEAN PANEL. MID. 17TH CENTURY
COURTESY OF VICTORIA & ALBERT MUSEUM, LONDON